MILWAUKEE

BREWERS

BY DAVID J. CLARKE

SportsZone

An Imprint of Abdo Publishing
abdobooks.com

abdobooks.com

Published by Abdo Publishing, a division of ABDO, PO Box 398166, Minneapolis, Minnesota 55439. Copyright © 2023 by Abdo Consulting Group, Inc. International copyrights reserved in all countries. No part of this book may be reproduced in any form without written permission from the publisher. SportsZone™ is a trademark and logo of Abdo Publishing.

Printed in China.
102022
012023

Cover Photo: Justin K. Aller/Getty Images Sport/Getty Images
Interior Photo: Morry Gash/AP Images, 4; Jonathan Daniel/Getty Images Sport/Getty Images, 6, 32, 38; Bettmann Archive/Getty Images, 9; Bettmann/Getty Images, 11; Louis Requena/Major League Baseball/Getty Images, 12; Focus on Sport/Getty Images, 14, 21; Rich Pilling/MLB Photos/Getty Images Sport/Getty Images, 16, 25; Ron Vesely/Getty Images Sport/Getty Images, 19; Ronald C. Modra/Getty Images Sport/Getty Images, 22, 28; Joe Robbins/Icon Sportswire/AP Images, 26; John Zich/AFP/Getty Images, 31; Nick Laham/Getty Images Sport/Getty Images, 34; Jim McIsaac/Getty Images Sport/Getty Images, 36; Nuccio DiNuzzo/Getty Images Sport/Getty Images, 41

Editor: Steph Giedd
Series Designer: Becky Daum

Library of Congress Control Number: 2022940492

Publisher's Cataloging-in-Publication Data

Names: Clarke, David J., author.
Title: Milwaukee Brewers / by David J. Clarke
Description: Minneapolis, Minnesota: Abdo Publishing, 2023 | Series: Inside MLB | Includes online resources and index.
Identifiers: ISBN 9781098290238 (lib. bdg.) | ISBN 9781098275433 (ebook)
Subjects: LCSH: Milwaukee Brewers (Baseball team)--Juvenile literature. | Baseball teams--Juvenile literature. | Professional sports--Juvenile literature. | Sports franchises--Juvenile literature. | Major League Baseball (Organization)--Juvenile literature.
Classification: DDC 796.35764--dc23

CONTENTS

BREW CREW

The Milwaukee Brewers traded four players to the Miami Marlins on January 25, 2018. In return, the Brewers picked up outfielder Christian Yelich. No one in Wisconsin knew what a steal the team had just received. Yelich had been a good player for five years, but not a great one. In Milwaukee he would blossom into one of the league's best.

That season the Brewers and Chicago Cubs had finished with identical 95–67 records. On October 1 they matched up at Chicago's Wrigley Field. A one-game playoff would decide the National League (NL) Central Division champion.

Yelich had just finished a Most Valuable Player (MVP) year. The spindly left-handed-hitting outfielder had set new career

Christian Yelich celebrates after hitting a home run late in the 2018 season.

The Brewers celebrate at Wrigley Field after defeating the Chicago Cubs in a one-game playoff for the 2018 NL Central Division title.

highs in nearly every offensive category. And his perfect swing had won him the NL batting title. He already had one hit on the day when he stepped into the batter's box in the top of the third. There were two outs in a scoreless game, but Milwaukee's Orlando Arcia stood on third. On a 1–1 pitch, Yelich smacked the ball up the middle to bring Arcia home. It was Yelich's 110th run batted in (RBI) of the season.

The Cubs eventually tied the game. But in the eighth inning, two Milwaukee runs broke the deadlock. Star closer Josh Hader then finished off the Cubs, and the Brewers had their first division title in seven years. Yelich finished the game 3-for-4 with an RBI and a stolen base.

It was the start of a run that would take Milwaukee within a game of the World Series. Yelich might look skinny at 6 feet, 3 inches and 195 pounds. But he had enough strength to carry a franchise on his back.

BRINGING IT BACK

Success has not come easy for Milwaukee. But in the mid-1960s, baseball fans in Wisconsin didn't care. They just wanted a team back.

Milwaukee had always been a baseball town. The original Milwaukee Brewers had been

BASEBALL'S PIONEERING WOMEN

After the outbreak of World War II (1939–45), professional baseball took a hit with several stars fighting overseas. The sport carried on in new ways, however. One idea was the All-American Girls Professional Baseball League, a pro league for women. Three of its teams played in southeast Wisconsin. The Racine Belles won the first league title in 1943, and the Milwaukee Chicks won the next year before folding. The Kenosha Comets also played nine seasons in the league, which lasted until 1954.

one of the founding members of the American League (AL) in 1901. But that franchise was gone after just one season. For the next 51 years, a minor league version of the Brewers entertained Milwaukee fans. That lasted until 1952, when the majors came back. The Braves moved in from Boston in 1953. Led by sluggers Hank Aaron and Eddie Mathews and the pitching of lefty Warren Spahn, the Milwaukee Braves were an elite team. They won a thrilling World Series in 1957 and reached another Fall Classic in 1958.

However, by 1966 the Braves were gone to Atlanta. The city's disappointment extended to one of the Braves' minority owners. Allan "Bud" Selig quickly put together an organization dedicated to bringing baseball back to his home state. He leaned on Milwaukee's baseball history and selected "Milwaukee Brewers Baseball Club" for the group's name.

PILOT PROGRAM

Selig's plan didn't work. Major League Baseball (MLB) expanded by four teams in the late 1960s.

BALL FOUR

The only season of the Seattle Pilots was chronicled in the groundbreaking book *Ball Four*. The memoir about his real experiences was written by one of the team's pitchers, Jim Bouton. While fans flocked to it, those around baseball hated Bouton's book. He told many private clubhouse stories and tales of players' off-field behavior. Bouton became an outcast in baseball, but the book remains widely read.

But Milwaukee wasn't selected. Instead, NL teams went to San Diego and Montreal. Kansas City, which had also lost a team in the late-1960s, rejoined the AL along with a team in Seattle.

The Kansas City Royals and the other three teams lobbied to join MLB in 1969. While three of the four new teams were initially successful, the Seattle Pilots were a mess. Seattle didn't have enough time to update its poor stadium, among other problems.

Prior to becoming the MLB commissioner, Bud Selig was best known for owning the Pilots/Brewers franchise.

The results were a disaster. The Pilots struggled on the field to a 64–98 record in the AL, and no one came out to watch them. Fewer than 700,000 fans turned up during the year. The team lost so much money that its owners were nearly bankrupt after one season. They needed to sell quickly. Selig saw another chance for Milwaukee.

MAD DASH TO MILWAUKEE

Selig agreed to buy the Pilots in the fall of 1969. But the negotiations dragged on for months. In March 1970, the Pilots' players reported to spring training not knowing where the team might play. The team's equipment and uniforms eventually ended up in Provo, Utah. There, the truck drivers were waiting for someone to tell them which city to drive toward.

Finally, on April 1, the Pilots were officially declared bankrupt. Selig finally had his team, but now he had no time. Opening Day of the 1970 season was just six days away.

Selig wanted the team to wear navy blue and red. Those had been the colors of the minor league Milwaukee Brewers. Instead, he had to take the Pilots' jerseys and quickly change the logos. As a result, Milwaukee's new Brewers took the field on April 7 at the city's County Stadium wearing Seattle's yellow and blue. Despite being second choice, the colors stuck.

Even on short notice, a crowd of more than 36,000 showed up for Milwaukee's opening game. But even with the support of the home crowd, the team failed to deliver. Brewers starting pitcher Lew Krausse lasted only three innings against the visiting California Angels. Milwaukee never figured out California starter Andy Messersmith. The righty struck out 11 Brewers over nine innings. The final score was an embarrassing

Versatile fielder Tommy Harper was an All-Star in his first season as a Brewer in 1970.

12–0 drubbing for Milwaukee. It didn't get much better the rest of the season, as the Brewers finished 65–97.

Better days would be ahead for the new, hastily assembled team in Milwaukee. But in getting there, the Brewers would soon test their fans' patience.

CHAPTER 2

BOMBERS AND BANGERS

Things calmed down for the Brewers after the wild start to their first season. But one thing did not change. For the first several years of the team's existence, Milwaukee did a lot of losing.

Though the team had some early stars, like outfielder Tommy Harper and first baseman George Scott, Milwaukee didn't reach 70 wins until 1973. That year a 74–88 record put Milwaukee 23 games out of first place.

The next season brought a fresh face to the Brewers. Shortstop Robin Yount was the team's top draft pick in 1973. He made the Opening Day roster in 1974 when he was still 18 years old. Just six games into his big-league career, Yount hit

Robin Yount joined the Brewers as an 18-year-old and played his entire 20-year career in Milwaukee.

Hank Aaron retired as the all-time major league leader in RBIs with 2,297.

a game-winning home run. It was just a glimpse of what was to come for the future star.

While Yount provided a look at Milwaukee's baseball future, the 1975 season brought one of the city's legends back. Hank Aaron began his MLB career with the old Milwaukee Braves in 1954. He stayed with the team for 21 years, sticking with the franchise when it moved to Atlanta. In 1974 he passed Babe Ruth to become the league's all-time home run king. But after the 1974 season, Aaron asked for a trade back to Milwaukee. The AL had recently introduced the designated hitter. That meant the 40-year-old Aaron could keep hitting without having to wear his legs out in the field.

Aaron stayed with the Brewers for two seasons. After the 1976 campaign, he retired with 755 home runs. That remained the MLB record until 2007. His presence in Milwaukee helped sell a few more tickets. But the Brewers had losing records both years he was there.

The Brewers were having trouble getting fans during the 1970 season. In late June, a 69-year-old supporter named Milt Mason decided to camp out on top of the scoreboard until the team drew 40,000 fans to a game. It finally happened on August 16, and Mason came down. Three years later, the Brewers took Mason's idea and created Bernie Brewer, the team's mascot who also "lived" at the ballpark.

BAMBI'S BOMBERS

By 1978 the Brewers were young and talented. Yount, now 22, was growing into a star. The team's farm system was starting to produce other talent. Outfielder Sixto Lezcano was in his fourth season and hit 21 homers. Center fielder Gorman Thomas was in his fifth year. He broke out with a career-high 32 dingers. And playing next to Yount at second base was 21-year-old rookie Paul Molitor.

Lefty Mike Caldwell tossed a major league–leading 23 complete games during his second season with the Brewers in 1978.

Over the next few seasons, the team's front office made some moves to enhance the Brewers roster. General manager Jim Baumer had made a deal with the Cincinnati Reds during the 1977 season for pitcher Mike Caldwell. The intense lefthander became the team's ace. One writer described Caldwell as "ornery, obnoxious, nasty, and downright mean." As a joke, he was given the nickname "Mr. Warmth." The next season, new manager Harry Dalton either signed or traded for several veterans to round out the lineup in 1978. Previously signed first baseman Cecil Cooper and newly signed outfielder Ben Oglivie were both power threats to complement Caldwell's defensive efforts on the mound.

Caldwell didn't grab the only good nickname in Milwaukee. The Brewers had a new manager that year, George Bamberger. Because the team hit a lot of home runs, the press dubbed Milwaukee "Bambi's Bombers." That power hitting, and Caldwell's nasty pitching, pushed the Brewers to 93 wins. But in the competitive AL East division, that wasn't good enough to make the playoffs.

A POSTSEASON TASTE

Despite 95 wins in 1979, the Brewers again missed out. Then the team hit some bad luck before the 1980 season. Bamberger suffered a heart attack in spring training. He missed the season's first two months before returning in June. But he didn't finish the year. The popular Bamberger, who often tailgated with fans after games, resigned in September.

Bamberger's replacement was Buck Rodgers, who had filled in during their leader's recovery. Rodgers oversaw the season from start to finish in 1981. It was a strange year in baseball. A strike halfway through the season interrupted play. As a result, the season was split into two halves. The division winner in each half went to the playoffs. As second-half champions, the Brewers met the New York Yankees in the AL Division Series (ALDS). Milwaukee fell behind 2–0 in the best-of-five playoff before battling back to win the next two games in New York.

The Brewers had a 2–0 lead in Game 5 at Yankee Stadium.
But the Yankees rallied back to win the game 7–3 and take
the series.

HARVEY'S WALLBANGERS

The Brewers started slowly in 1982. In early June, they were
just 23–24. Dalton fired Rodgers and hired Harvey Kuenn as the
new manager. The laid-back former big-league infielder and
outfielder was a perfect fit. The Brewers went 72–43 the rest of
the season to reach the playoffs again.

Milwaukee once again had a thumping lineup. Cooper,
Oglivie, Yount, Thomas, and catcher Ted Simmons all hit more
than 20 homers. Molitor, now playing third base, added 19
more. Yount was also the AL MVP. The team became known as
"Harvey's Wallbangers."

However, the Brewers weren't just offense. Caldwell was still
a star, winning 17 games. Reliever Rollie Fingers had won the
AL Cy Young Award as the league's top pitcher in 1981. In 1982
starter Pete Vuckovich won it after finishing 18–6. The Brewers
also traded for 37-year-old righty Don Sutton during the
season. He came up big on the final day of the year. Milwaukee
was tied with the Baltimore Orioles, and the two teams squared
off with the AL East title on the line. Baltimore had already
won the first three games of the series to pull even. But Sutton

Slugging first baseman Cecil Cooper led the league in doubles and RBIs twice each in his 11 years with the Brewers.

saved the day with eight strong innings. Yount hit two of the Brewers' four homers in a 10–2 clinching victory.

There was more drama in the playoffs as Milwaukee faced the California Angels in the AL Championship Series (ALCS). The Brewers lost the first two games in California but won the next two back home. Milwaukee trailed in the deciding fifth game. It was 3–2 in the bottom of the seventh when the team loaded the bases with two outs. Cooper stepped up and ripped a

single to left to score Charlie Moore and Jim Gantner. The lead
held, and the Brewers were on their way to the World Series for
the first time.

POWER VS. SPEED

The Brewers rode their big bats to the World Series. Their
opponents, the St. Louis Cardinals, got there with their legs.
St. Louis was last in MLB with 67 homers, while the Brewers had
a league-best 216. The Cardinals scored runs by stealing bases
and playing small ball. The contrast in styles was the big story
heading into the series.

The Wallbangers rocked St. Louis with 17 hits in Game 1,
winning 10–0. But the Cardinals won the next two. The seesaw
battle then tipped back to the Brewers. A six-run seventh
inning won Game 4 by a score of 7–5. A Yount homer
highlighted a 6–4 win in Game 5.

Milwaukee went back to St. Louis with a chance to claim a
title. The veteran Sutton took the mound but didn't make it out
of the fifth inning. In a twist, it was the Cardinals who homered
twice in a 13–1 rout.

A home run by Oglivie helped Milwaukee take a 3–1 lead in
Game 7. But Vuckovich was pitching with a torn rotator cuff, a
part of his shoulder joint, and hit the wall in the sixth inning.
He gave up two hits before giving way to reliever Bob McClure.

Paul Molitor set a World Series record by getting five hits in one game on October 12, 1982.

The lefty walked a batter, loading the bases. Then he gave up two singles and lost the lead.

Tensions nearly boiled over in the seventh. Pitching for the Cardinals was ace Joaquín Andújar, who liked to taunt hitters after he got them out. He retired Gantner to end the seventh inning, and the two nearly attacked each other. Home plate umpire Lee Weyer had to haul Andújar away. After that, St. Louis manager Whitey Herzog brought in Bruce Sutter to finish the game. The Brewers couldn't get a ball out of the infield against one of the league's best closers. St. Louis won 6–3 to end Milwaukee's championship dreams.

THE LOST YEARS

The Brewers had to play the 1983 season without their two Cy Young winners. Pete Vuckovich made three appearances for the Brewers, but his torn rotator cuff had to heal. And Rollie Fingers had a torn muscle in his forearm. The rest of the staff struggled, and the bats couldn't carry the team. Milwaukee slipped to fifth place. A year later, the Brewers lost 94 games.

It was the first of three straight losing seasons. Even the return of manager George Bamberger couldn't turn things around. He resigned again with nine games left in the 1986 season. Under new manager Tom Trebelhorn, the Brewers got back to a winning record in 1987. Through the 1992 season,

Pitcher Pete Vuckovich had a role in the 1989 movie *Major League* as Clu Haywood, the New York Yankees' enemy batter opposite of Cleveland's relief pitcher, played by Charlie Sheen.

Milwaukee had just one losing year. However, none of those records were good enough to win the AL East.

THE BIG THREE

By the early 1990s, Milwaukee's roster had changed quite a bit. But three players remained from the team's glory years. Robin Yount had first appeared in the big leagues in 1974. Jim Gantner made his debut in 1976. Two years later, Paul Molitor first put on a Brewers uniform.

By the end of 1992, all three had played more than 1,800 games in Milwaukee. Molitor had led the league in runs, hits, doubles, and triples during different seasons in his Milwaukee career. Gantner was a steady contact hitter who could play all over the infield.

However, Yount was the Brewers' iconic player. As he had joined the league at age 18, he was still only 36 in 1992. That September he became the third-youngest player to join baseball's 3,000-hit club. Only Braves legend Hank Aaron and former Detroit Tigers great Ty Cobb were younger when they hit that mark.

The 1992 season was the last time all three played together. Gantner retired. Molitor, who was still one of the game's best hitters, signed with the Toronto Blue Jays. And the 1993 season was Yount's last. He retired as one of baseball's most

Second baseman Jim Gantner looks to turn a double play against the California Angels during the 1982 season.

underappreciated stars. Despite 20 years that saw him win the MVP Award twice, Yount made only three All-Star teams in his career.

BERNIE AND BOB

With Molitor, Gantner, and Yount no longer around, the losses piled up. Starting in 1993, the Brewers put out 12 losing teams in a row. The Brewers needed other ideas to get fans to the ballpark.

Bernie Brewer perches in his chalet in left-center field at American Family Field.

Milwaukee was still an entertaining place to watch a game. One of the biggest reasons was the team's popular mascot, Bernie Brewer. Bernie started in the 1970s as a live person. He "lived" in a chalet in the left-field bleachers with his wife, Bonnie Brewer. Bernie would ride down a slide into a mug after every Milwaukee home run and win. Bonnie only lasted until 1979, and in 1984, a sound tower replaced Bernie's chalet during stadium renovations. The team retired the mascots.

That lasted until 1993, when fans pressured the Brewers into bringing Bernie back. This time he was a costumed mascot. He moved back into his left-field home and stayed there when the team moved into Miller Park (now known as American Family Field) in 2001.

When Bernie slides at games now, he does it under a light-up sign reading "Get up! Get up! Get outta here!" That is the famous home run call of Milwaukee radio announcer Bob Uecker. A former major league catcher, Uecker became the voice of the Brewers in 1971. By the time the team was successful in the early 1980s, Uecker was one of the game's most popular announcers.

In addition to calling the game well, Uecker stood out for his sense of humor. He often made fun of his own short playing

THE SAUSAGE RACE

Another key element of entertainment at Brewers games is the sausage race. Starting in the early 1990s, a cartoon sausage race was played on the scoreboard during certain games. In 2000 the race became a live event with runners racing around the outfield in Polish sausage, bratwurst, Italian sausage, and hot dog suits. In 2007 a fifth racer, in a chorizo costume, was added. Today the contestants are known as the "Famous Racing Sausages."

Sportscaster, comedian, actor, and former MLB player Bob Uecker was nicknamed "Mr. Baseball" by TV talk show host Johnny Carson.

career with quotes like "I knew my career was over. In 1965 my baseball card came out with no picture."

His entertaining style soon made Uecker a wanted man in the TV and film industries. He was already a veteran of TV commercials when he got a starring role on a sitcom in the late 1980s called *Mr. Belvedere*. He also starred in the baseball comedy *Major League* and its two sequels. The films centered on fictional versions of MLB teams. Uecker played wisecracking announcer Harry Doyle.

Despite his fame, Uecker continued to work for the Brewers. In 2003 he won the Ford C. Frick Award for excellence in broadcasting. As of 2022, he had been on the air for 51 years.

SWITCHING IT UP

Despite having great entertainment on the radio and in the park, the Brewers were struggling in the 1990s. But team owner Bud Selig was becoming extremely popular with those who ran other baseball teams. In 1992 he started acting as the league's commissioner. He didn't officially have the job and continued to own the Brewers. But after five years in both roles, he was hired by the league full-time. This meant giving up the Brewers. The team was turned over to his daughter Wendy.

Bud Selig oversaw two rounds of expansion to the majors. In 1993 the Colorado Rockies and Florida Marlins both joined the NL. Five years later, MLB was set to add the Arizona Diamondbacks to the NL and Tampa Bay Rays (then called the Devil Rays) to the AL. But adding one franchise to each league would create an odd number of teams. For scheduling purposes, those numbers had to be even. That meant that one team would have to switch.

Before the Brewers, Milwaukee had been an NL town with the Braves. But Selig didn't want to look like he was favoring his old team. So, he asked the Kansas City Royals first.

When Kansas City said no, Milwaukee made the switch. The move made history. The Brewers were the first team ever to move from one major league to the other.

ALL-STAR DISASTER

In 2002 Milwaukee was still in the MLB basement. The Brewers' farm system struggled to turn out any talented players at all. But the Brewers had built a new stadium the year before, and now superstars from all 30 MLB teams were coming to Milwaukee for the 2002 All-Star Game.

For decades, the All-Star Game was hotly contested. Since the AL and NL teams never played each other, pride was on the line when the stars met for the midseason exhibition game. However, when the arrival of interleague play began in 1997, AL and NL teams met during the regular season. The All-Star Game became more for show.

The fun ran out at the 2002 game in Milwaukee. After 11 innings, the two leagues were tied 7–7. That was a problem, since neither team had any pitchers left. No one wanted to wear out a superstar at the All-Star Game, so Selig decided on the field to call the game off. It would end in a tie. The decision angered many and led to several All-Star rule changes to make sure it would never happen again. The biggest switch was that the winner of the game would get home-field advantage in

Bud Selig, *center*, discusses whether to end the 2002 All-Star Game in a 7–7 tie due to the lack of remaining pitchers.

the World Series. That rule stood until it was scrapped for the 2017 season.

While the 2002 All-Star Game was a low point for baseball, it wasn't the worst thing to happen to the Brewers that year. They finished the season 56–106. It was the worst record in team history. And fans in Milwaukee weren't sure it would ever get better.

Brewers
49

CHAPTER 4

REVIVAL

Shortly after the 2002 season ended, the Brewers hired Ned Yost to be their new manager. While it took several years to rebuild the team, hiring Yost was the first step. It wasn't the only big change. In 2004 the Brewers were put up for sale. Banker Mark Attanasio completed his purchase before the 2005 season. That year was the first time a Selig had not owned the Brewers since the team moved from Seattle.

Attanasio had a lot of work to do to win over fans. One goodwill move he made was to give every ticket away for free to the final home game of the 2005 season. But what Brewers fans wanted most was a winning team.

Right-hander Yovani Gallardo pitched for the Brewers from 2007 to 2014.

Corey Hart slides into third during a 2009 game against the New York Mets.

SOMETHING BREWING

That took a few more years. But in 2007, Milwaukee trotted out another young, exciting lineup, just like it had in the late 1970s. Infielders Rickie Weeks, J. J. Hardy, Ryan Braun, and Prince Fielder were all 23 or 24 years old. Power-hitting outfielder Corey Hart was only 25. On the mound, exciting rookie Yovani Gallardo joined 28-year-old starter Ben Sheets.

The Brewers had an 8 1/2 game lead in June, but the young team threw it away down the stretch. Yost took most of the blame from the media but kept his job.

The next season, he wasn't so lucky. The Brewers were 80–56 when August ended and looking good to earn the NL wild-card spot in the postseason. Then they lost 15 of their next 19 games. During that stretch, Yost was fired. Third base coach Dale Sveum, a former Brewers player, took over with 12 games left.

However, it was a pitcher that came over in a midseason trade who saved the day. CC Sabathia was picked up from Cleveland in July. In the final two weeks of the season, the lefty started three games. He won the last two, including a complete game on the final day of the season. Braun backed him up with a tiebreaking two-run homer in the eighth inning as Milwaukee won 3–1. The win, combined with a loss by the New York Mets, ended the Brewers' long playoff drought.

By the time the Brewers got a home game in the playoffs, they were down 2–0 to the Philadelphia Phillies in the NL Division Series (NLDS). In Miller Park, the Brewers won 4–1

BRAUN'S MVP

Brewers outfielder Ryan Braun won the 2011 NL MVP Award after hitting .332 with 33 home runs and 111 RBIs. The next year, he hit 41 homers. But halfway through the 2013 season, Braun was suspended for using performance-enhancing drugs. Many people around baseball thought Braun should forfeit his 2011 award. He didn't, but Braun never played as well again. He hit 30 homers only once more in his career, which ran until 2020.

J. J. Hardy gets a hit in Game 3 of the 2008 NLDS against the Philadelphia Phillies.

behind three hits from Hardy. Philadelphia ended the series the next day, but the future looked bright in Wisconsin.

PLAYOFF FEVER

Sabathia's stay in Milwaukee was short. He left after the 2008 season and signed as a free agent with the New York Yankees. He was tough to replace, and the Brewers had losing records each of the next two years.

They bounced back in a big way in 2011, winning 96 games. That was the most in team history, one more than the 1982 World Series team. And that wasn't the only similarity to 1982. There was plenty of playoff drama as well.

The NLDS came down to a decisive Game 5 against the Arizona Diamondbacks. But Milwaukee had suffered two straight heavy losses. Arizona came back in the deciding game at Miller Park as well, erasing a 2–1 Milwaukee lead in the top of the ninth. That sent the game into extra innings. And another new pickup became the star for Milwaukee.

Early in the year, the Brewers had traded for Nyjer Morgan. Prior to playing in the majors, the confident outfielder gave himself the unusual nickname "Tony Plush," which he then began going by on the field. But he was having a bad series. Through the first four games, Morgan hit just 1-for-11. Then he wiped away the bad memories in the 10th inning. Batting with

Nyjer Morgan celebrates after getting the game-winning RBI in Game 5 of the 2011 NLDS.

one out and Carlos Gómez on second base, Morgan socked a single to center. The speedy Gómez came around to score. Milwaukee celebrated a playoff series win for the first time since the 1982 ALCS.

That set up an NL Championship Series (NLCS) matchup with their 1982 World Series opponent, the St. Louis Cardinals. The switch to the NL had made the teams division rivals.

The Brewers fell behind in each of the first four games. But they rallied from 5–2 down to win Game 1. In Game 4, Milwaukee erased a 2–0 deficit to win 4–2.

All year long, Milwaukee had been a solid pitching team. But in the final two games, the Cardinals thumped the Brewers' staff. St. Louis outscored Milwaukee 19–7 to take the series in six games.

PITCHING RICH

One of the Brewers' backup infielders in 2011 was Craig Counsell. It was the 40-year-old's final MLB season. Four years later, he returned to Milwaukee as the team's new manager in early May after the Brewers got off to a 7–18 start. The Brewers had been struggling and had missed the playoffs each year since their NLCS run in 2011. Not much changed at first. Milwaukee lost 94 games in Counsell's first year. However, things would turn around soon enough.

Before the 2018 season, team general manager David Stearns pulled off a big trade. He sent several minor leaguers to the Miami Marlins for outfielder Christian Yelich. The left-hander won the league MVP right away while leading Milwaukee's offense.

Milwaukee's other strength in 2018 was its pitching staff. Three pitchers had at least 10 saves. Righties Corey Knebel and Jeremy Jeffress combined for more than 170 strikeouts. But the Brewers' biggest weapon was 6-foot-3-inch lefty Josh Hader. The long-haired reliever was

RED HOT HADER

On May 8, 2021, Josh Hader recorded his 400th strikeout. He became the fastest pitcher in MLB history to reach that mark. Later that year, Hader started a streak of 40 straight appearances without allowing a run. That streak tied an MLB record before it finally ended on June 7, 2022.

nearly unhittable. He struck out 143 batters in 81 1/3 innings.
For that performance, he was named the NL's Reliever of
the Year.

Milwaukee still needed a one-game playoff to beat the
Chicago Cubs for the Brewers' third-ever division title. From
there it was on to the playoffs, where the Brewers made quick
work of the Colorado Rockies. After a walk-off win in Game 1,
Milwaukee shut the Rockies out in two straight games.

Milwaukee had a 2–1 lead on the Los Angeles Dodgers
in the NLCS after three tight contests. Game 4 was another
close one. The teams dueled to a 1–1 tie into the 13th inning.
Both were running out of pitchers. Finally, Los Angeles won
the game on a walk-off single in the bottom of the inning off
Brewers righty Junior Guerra.

The teams battled to a seventh game. Down 2–1 in the top
of the seventh inning, Jeffress gave up a three-run homer to
the Dodgers' Yasiel Puig. Milwaukee couldn't recover and came
up just short of the World Series again.

BUILT TO LAST

Unlike previous playoff teams, these Brewers were good
enough to keep returning to the postseason. The Brewers
made it back to the playoffs each of the next three years. But
winning proved tougher. They lost in the NL wild-card round

Pitcher Corbin Burnes led the majors with a 2.43 earned-run average during his Cy Young Award–winning 2021 season.

in 2019 and 2020. A division title allowed them to skip that round in 2021. But the Brewers won only one game in the NLDS against the Atlanta Braves.

Still, the Brewers were set up for success. Hader remained one of the game's best relievers. And righty Corbin Burnes claimed the NL Cy Young Award in 2021. He was the first Brewer to win it since 1982. Brewers fans hoped the individual awards would soon lead to another championship season in Milwaukee.

TIMELINE

1969

The franchise begins play as the Seattle Pilots but lasts only one season.

1970

The sale of the Brewers to Bud Selig is finalized just six days before Opening Day. The team moves to Milwaukee and finishes 65–97.

1973

Mascot Bernie Brewer moves into his home in left-center field.

1974

Robin Yount debuts for the Brewers at age 18, beginning a 20-year career with the team.

1975

Hank Aaron plays the first of two seasons with the Brewers, returning to Milwaukee after beginning his career there 21 years earlier with the city's former team, the Braves.

1978

The "Bambi's Bombers" Milwaukee lineup powers the team to its first winning record but finishes short of the playoffs.

1981

The Brewers reach the playoffs for the first time before losing to the New York Yankees in the ALDS.

1982

Milwaukee reaches its first World Series, a seven-game loss to the St. Louis Cardinals.

1992

After the 1992 season, Jim Gantner retires after 17 seasons with the Brewers, and Paul Molitor leaves the team as a free agent.

1993

Yount retires as the Brewers' all-time leader in several offensive categories, including games played, hits, and home runs.

1998

The Brewers become the first team to move from one major league to the other when they switch from the AL to the NL.

2002

The Brewers finish 56–106, the worst record in team history.

2008

CC Sabathia's complete game on the final day of the season clinches the NL wild card for Milwaukee, the team's first playoff appearance since 1982.

2011

The Brewers win the NL Central but lose to the Cardinals in the NLCS.

2018

Milwaukee wins 96 games for the second time in team history but loses a seven-game NLCS to the Los Angeles Dodgers.

2021

Right-hander Corbin Burnes becomes the first Milwaukee Cy Young Award winner since Pete Vuckovich in 1982 as the Brewers win their fourth division title.

TEAM FACTS

FRANCHISE HISTORY

Seattle Pilots (1969)
Milwaukee Brewers (1970–)

KEY PLAYERS

Ryan Braun (2007–20)
Corbin Burnes (2018–)
Mike Caldwell (1977–84)
Cecil Cooper (1977–87)
Prince Fielder (2005–11)
Rollie Fingers (1981–85)
Jim Gantner (1976–92)
Geoff Jenkins (1998–07)
Paul Molitor (1978–92)
Don Money (1973–83)
Ben Oglivie (1978–86)
Ben Sheets (2001–08)
Ted Simmons (1981–85)
Gorman Thomas (1973–76, 1978–83, 1986)
Pete Vuckovich (1981–86)
Christian Yelich (2018–)
Robin Yount (1974–93)

KEY MANAGERS

George Bamberger (1978–80, 1985–86)
Craig Counsell (2015–)
Harvey Kuenn (1975, 1982–83)

HOME STADIUMS

Sick's Stadium (1969)
Milwaukee County Stadium (1970–2000)
American Family Field (2001–)
Also known as:
Miller Park (2001–21)

SAUSAGE SCANDAL

In 2003 Pittsburgh Pirates first baseman Randall Simon was arrested after lightly bonking one of the Miller Park sausage racers on the head with a bat as the costumed runner ran by. Simon was cited for disorderly conduct and fined more than $400. He was also suspended three games and fined by MLB. Later that season, when Simon returned to Milwaukee as a member of the Chicago Cubs, teammates jokingly held him back as the sausage racers passed.

THE STREAK

Paul Molitor put together a 39-game hitting streak in 1987, ranking seventh in MLB history. When the streak ended, Molitor was in the on-deck circle in the bottom of the tenth inning. Rick Manning, batting ahead of Molitor, hit a walk-off single to win the game. Milwaukee fans booed Manning for the hit, since Molitor didn't get a chance to bat.

LITTLE BIG LEAGUE

Across the parking lot from American Family Field sits Helfaer Field, a little league stadium that cost $3.1 million to build. The field occupies the same space that the Brewers' old park, County Stadium, once did.

DIVISION RIVALS

In addition to switching leagues, the Brewers are the only MLB team that has played in four different divisions. They have played in the AL West, East, and Central, as well as the NL Central.

GLOSSARY

ace

A team's best starting pitcher.

bankrupt

Unable to pay debts due to lack of money.

closer

A pitcher who comes in at the end of the game to secure a win for his team.

commissioner

The chief executive of a sports league.

exhibition

A game that doesn't count in the standings.

expansion

The addition of new teams to increase the size of a league.

farm system

In baseball, all the minor league teams that feed players to one major league team.

franchise

A sports organization, including the top-level team and all minor league affiliates.

free agent

A player whose rights are not owned by any team.

save

When a relief pitcher comes in to finish a close game and secures a win.

tailgate

To gather outside a stadium, often with food served from the back of a parked vehicle.

walk-off

Any victory in which the home team scores the winning run in the bottom of the final inning.

MORE INFORMATION

BOOKS

Flynn, Brendan. *The MLB Encyclopedia*. Minneapolis, MN: Abdo Publishing, 2022.

Hewson, Anthony K. *GOATs of Baseball*. Minneapolis, MN: Abdo Publishing, 2022.

Mitchell, Bo. *Ultimate MLB Road Trip*. Minneapolis, MN: Abdo Publishing, 2019.

ONLINE RESOURCES

To learn more about the Milwaukee Brewers, please visit **abdobooklinks.com** or scan this QR code. These links are routinely monitored and updated to provide the most current information available.

INDEX

ABOUT THE AUTHOR

David J. Clarke is a freelance writer. Originally from Helena, Montana, he now lives in Savannah, Georgia, with his golden retriever, Gus.